Paradise Anonymous

Paradise Anonymous

poems
by Oriana Ivy

MOON
TIDE PRESS

~ 2023 ~

Editor-in-chief
Eric Morago

Editor Emeritus
Michael Miller

Marketing Specialist
Ellen Webre

Proofreader
LeAnne Hunt

Front cover art
Charles Sherman

Book design
Michael Wada & Jeremy Ra

Moon Tide logo design
Abraham Gomez

Paradise Anonymous
is published by Moon Tide Press

Moon Tide Press
6709 Washington Ave. #9297
Whittier, CA 90608
www.moontidepress.com

FIRST EDITION

Printed in the United States of America

ISBN # 978-1-957799-11-7

Contents

I.

The Immortalist

Key to the World

I stand in front of the mirror,
trying to place everything
correctly: tip of tongue against

upper teeth, right hand checking
vibrations of the larynx.
"This is your key to the world,"

states my *English for Today*,
a book of secrets where Tom and Jane
carry on their cracked romance:

Tom, is this a girl?
No, this is a lamp.

I rehearse the sacred chant:
Thelma threw thistles
through the thick of her thumb.

Thistle while you work!
A tooth for a truth,
a thigh for an eye!

"They lisp," the teacher
explains. "Maybe because
of cold wind."

"Your r's are too guttural,"
teacher warns. Guttural,
that's me. What's the meaning

of *the*, I ask. Where's the tip
of your foreign tongue?
Between Thelma's teeth.

Tom, is this a mouth?
No, this is a hoof.

Today the *the*. Tomorrow
I open the world.

Military Preparedness

We marched around the schoolyard,
memorized rifle parts.
In June we were taken
to an indoor shooting range.

I pulled the trigger blindly,
shaken by the noise, the recoil.
Most of the time
I hit the side wall.

I pleaded poor eyesight,
was excused.
In truth I didn't know
how to sight the target.

*

Grenade training: if you throw
a grenade to your right, you must run
to your left. I never got as far
as that. My fate was sealed in first grade

when I switched our primers
while a classmate was away
from our desk. *My* copy
had crisper, darker print. To be different

was to be wrong.
Someone else's meant *superior*.
I felt guilty about it for years.
I failed to confess it in church,

and felt guilty about that
also. At ten I confessed,
knees sunk into the hollowed,
creaky kneeling board,

the air musty with so many sins.
The priest solemnly insisted
I must give the primer back.
Also say five Hail Marys

and three Our Fathers. By then
I lived in another town,
on the verge of suspecting
both life and afterlife were absurd.

*

There's a New Age theory of the beyond:
we get to see our lives
moment by moment all over again.
What an economical design for hell.

But I wouldn't beg for another
chance to do it right.
Impossible. I'd like to fail again,
in a brilliant new way.

I'd like an angel to be
not a giant like my six-foot-six
Military Preparedness instructor, but a small
lap angel. He wouldn't force me

to review my life
or scores on the shooting range.
He wouldn't care about rifle parts,
wouldn't listen to my "field report."

He'd take me by the hand and say,
*Relax, you unexpectedly
made it, here, eat this lily* —
and I'd eat it the wrong way,

as the first time I was given a banana,
and ate it sideways,
leaving behind a delicately carved
banana-core. And then we exit

laughing. You have to have
military preparedness for that.

Angel Envy

"What is it," the nun intones,
"that we envy angels?"
Angel-envying eight-year-olds,
we all shout, "Wings!"

"No, no, no," chimes the nun.
"Think about it: angels can see
God." We think about it.
We still want wings.

"And what is it," the nun presses on,
"that holy angels envy *us*?"
We squirm on the hard benches.
"Angels envy us our bodies."

We almost stop breathing.

*

"Angels are made of aura-like
material," a New-Age half-nun
gasps in a half-whisper.
"When two angels stand close,

their wings inter-penetrate."
I think of Milton's
Easier than Air with Air,
if spirits embrace, total they mix.

That's what I always wanted —
blind Milton, how did you
divine — beyond the startling
rose of genitals, entirely

entering each other.

*

If spirits embrace . . . .

But can angels croon *Mmmm* . . .
Later, can they lazily
disentangle themselves
to get up and go pee?

Virgin nun of my childhood,
many years late I raise my hand.
In your gray habit and unloved
black shoes,

how did you know
what the angels crave:
our bodies, soft as regret;
our laughter so much like pain.

*

Between dream and star,
we sleep like Jacob
on his pillow of stone.
I still think about it:

we don't want to see
God. We want wings.

A Failed Propaganda Meeting at Cinema Desire

Since earliest childhood we were told
the red in the Polish flag stood for blood.
Now on the stage, two colossal

bouquets of red gladioli.
In the haze of upward petals,
the balding propagandist blossoms:

Isn't the Soviet Union
the greatest, the most advanced,
the most democratic country in the world?

He raises his voice: "Let us
salute our brother: *Long live*
the Soviet Union!" He lifts his arms

like an orchestra conductor,
motioning us to respond with a choral
Long live! I move my lips

in a mute shout,
raising my chin to mime
the final vowel like a howl.

Long live! the political educator
strains at the top of his amplified voice —
along with a squeak

of a few voices from the front row.
I look around: my classmates are
moving their lips without making a sound.

The theater is filled with classes
from several schools —
more than three hundred students.

The propagandist shouts even louder,
Long live the Soviet Union!
Again the upsweep of his arms.

This time a stumbling chorus
of six or seven voices.
Once more the educator tries

to rouse us to the correct zeal —
then shrugs — then strides —
then breaks into a run

toward the side door.
The wind of his retreat
barely musses the heavy gladioli.

All Souls

Sometimes I think Warsaw fog
is the dead, coming back

to seek their old homes —
wanting to touch even the walls.

But they cannot find those walls,
so they embrace the trees instead,

lindens and enduring chestnuts;
they embrace the whole city,

lay their arms around the bridges
and the droplet-beaded street lamps;

they pray in the Square of Three Crosses,
kneel among the candles and flowers

under bronze plaques that say
On this spot, 100 people were shot —

they bow, they kiss
even the railroad tracks —

they do not complain, only hold
what they can, in unraveling white.

An Apple Tree for Osip Mandelstam

My animal, my age, who will be able
to look into your eyes?
— O. M.

You keep returning, Osip Mandelstam.
You flash across the Siberian night,
the arc of your body thrown

into a common grave,
before the ground was frozen,
somewhere between birch stumps.

You wash outside in the dark,
black water in the barrel
salted with stars and the truth.

You keep returning to ask,
Why has the music stopped?
Why is there such silence?

*

In your eyes, unerasable archives:
the century of the hyena,
spastic laughter of the machine guns;

the century of the bored clerk
who writes down names,
and crosses some out.

Come live in the apple tree
in front of my window.
For you I want summer,

the ripening light.
Don't think about the clouds
bloodied with sunset.

Three Women

Walked into autumn, in a mountain
village at night. The youngest,
the beautiful one, said,
"Let's lie down and look at the stars."

Oh speech beyond delight:
two women lying down
on the road, while the third
like a mother stood guard.

No star was withheld. A sky like that
needs to be seen lying down.
The pavement felt like a good
firm bed, neither cold nor hard.

In my childhood such wealth
was called a diamond night —
this dome of blazing darkness,
this vertigo of light.

And we were not afraid.
We lay open-eyed
while above us burned
the diamond city of time.

We could wish endless wishes,
but there was no need,
with such luxurious
light in our lives. We lay silent

in the silence of the stars,
letting the kingdom come.

Questions for God

I love deathbed stories.
Heisenberg allegedly said:
"I'm planning to pose
two questions to God:

why relativity, and why
chaos. I suspect
He'll be able to answer
the first one."

Most people aren't that deep.
Every day I prepare
a new question to pose to God,
though no doubt it's the same

question already asked
a trillion trillion times,
and in vain. All my life I have sought
a science-compatible God,

friendly and kidding around,
like scientists at a gerontology convention.
But the I-Am-That-I-Am
will speak to me neither

from a burning bush,
nor from the serpent space-time
curving back on itself —
In the neural branches

of my Tree of Knowledge,
I already suspect
God will have my mother's
face, and will greet me

in the doorway of a nebula
in her usual way:
"Take off that awful blouse at once,
and put on something pretty."

The Immortalist

In memory of Richard E. Lee, teacher and shaman

"I am in trouble with the school system
because I believe we are immortal,"
my old professor tells me,

the one who taught immortality
and creative writing.
Metaphysics washes off in the shower,

but not love for the body's baroque
nooks and notches, sneezes, belly growls —
the soul's helpless love

for the body's animal forgiveness.
Is that what he meant, this elf
in the graying nimbus?

I offered my wisdom of youth:
"Only our yearning is immortal,
Eros like an upswept flame" —

He scribbled: "Be more vulgar.
I'm a sucker for frustrated lipstick.
P.S. I hope you get laid."

*

He said, "Don't let dying
stop you from anything you love."
He died on winter solstice,

squeezing through the shortening daylight
into space-time not taught
by the school system. Before the

diagnosis, he dreamed about
a train wreck. And knew.
And ordered coffee and croissants.

*

I wanted to call him to say,
"Don't die. Be more vulgar."

But he was already
luminous, beyond distinction.

Jacaranda

A jacaranda undulates across
three wide windows uptown —
billowing and pressing,

thousands of greedy mouths
trying to reach through the glass
with moist little lilac snouts.

That's where God likes to be:
waterfalls, whirlwinds,
wildflowers waving

on the edge of the cliff —
God blowing kisses
from the abyss.

God receives countless prayers
from lovers and aging poets,
the guard in his guard-booth at night,

women who date only prisoners,
and other holy and unholy fools
trying to nail themselves to a cross.

The point of being on the cross
is to become a blossoming tree,
the God of the Jacaranda wants us

to see, waving in merciless
glory — showering lilac
jacaranda kisses

on you and me,
and the hard pavement below.

Our Lady of the Third Arm

Because you need two arms
to be a woman,
and one to reach for the fruit
from the Tree of Life.

Two to do cooking and laundry,
the third one to conduct
an orchestra of clouds.
Two to type, and the other one
to embroider the handkerchief of time.

The museum says the third arm
was painted in after the theft
of a votive offering made
by Saint John of Damascus.

Legends lie. Women know. Three
is the minimum design:
two to pick up a crying child,
and the third one to embrace yourself.

It's the worst handicap,
not having the third arm,
the one that grows in solitude.
The one that gathers twilight

and the birds' last chorale.
The one that waves goodbye,
while the other two
still serve food to the guests.

Our Lady in her crown of stars
is busy holding the divine —
but with the stolen third arm
she blesses us
from a golden Byzantine sky.

Adam's Language

I wake and dream: *What language am I in?*
Dazed with creation, he stares at me.
I tell him like a happy child:
I am in Adam's language.

My voice this morning has a higher pitch —
I recognize my cousin Zula's voice.
Across the ocean, mountains, graves,
she seems to ask, "Why don't you trust

the syllables you tasted first,
the tongues of wind over the Baltic dunes?"
But I want Adam, the yet unharmed
man in the Garden before the exile,

tendrils of fingers still divine.
Let's name again the animals.
Let's fish in the newborn river
for shiny silver vowels.

But Adam is forbidden —
we are the fruit of Eden,
our first language lost
like the face of the Unknown God.

The burning branches of I AM
will never speak to us again.
I grieve that I am homeless.
A larger self replies:

All languages are Adam's.
Beloved, you are home.

Daughter of the Church

The nun rustles, black robe,
the starched December of her headdress,
teaching a row of seven-year-olds
to kneel on the stone church floor
and beat our chests: *my fault, my fault,*

my most grievous fault.
She shows us colored slides
of the Crucifixion:
Each time you sin, you drive a nail
into the flesh of Jesus.

At eleven I confess to impurity.
With boys, with girls, or by yourself?
The question intrigues me.
The confessional gapes like a mildewed ear.
With a sinner's bravado I whisper,
With boys, with girls, and by myself.

After communion I cross my arms
to keep the miracle inside me.
I collect pocket pictures of the saints.
I pray to the Madonna of the Seven
Sorrows, seven swords thrust into her
delicately bleeding heart.

Holding a lit candle, repeating the novena,
I stand last in the row of girls.
Slow petitions of smoke uncurl
from the quivering flame tips.
Wax sweats opaque tears.
The priest looks so unhappy,

I fall in love with him.
God sees every thought
in my impure head.
The priest dips his fingers
in a gilded bowl,
and draws a cross of ash on my forehead.

Wheatchild

When I was so new I was let
run naked, I'd step
into wheat. The stalks closed
above my head.

Laughing I would enter
such a golden drowning.
Cornflowers. The sun
split into a thousand sheaves.

It sways above me still:
the soul has no past tense.
Laughing I step out,
a child clothed with the sun,

into the arms of the world.

Grandmother's Hairnets

Other grandmothers knitted.
Mine only crocheted.
And exclusively hairnets.

Ever since I was a toddler,
I remember her that way,
with a little silver hook,

spiraling around and around
the nothing at the top.
Endless hairnets!

She kept her hair short.
Even after eighty,
it was only beginning to gray.

Her hairnets were brown
or black, the yarn so fine
the hairnet hardly showed.

It was not about need.
It was about that spiraling
around empty space,

the eye of wisdom that opens
when you come to know
how in one moment

you can lose everything except
your soul. All else
is a ball of yarn.

It's about the flight
of the hook.

My First Love Wears Dentures

He moves into my house. On the way
to the bathroom to shave, he takes out
his teeth. In the dream, we're as easy
together as an old married couple.

At thirteen, I'd almost faint if he
stood near — after such trembling
passion, surely he should leave me
more than just his dentures.

He closes the bathroom door. I knock,
bringing him fresh towels.
All those years it might as well
have been him — a woman's endless

work of love: bringing
clean towels, tenderness.
I walk into the bathroom. He shrinks
and travels backward, a web of cracks

at the border of childhood and youth.
Like Penelope I unravel the navy-blue
sweater he wore in high school.
"Love, where are you going?" I call.

I can no longer see his face.
I can no longer tell, is it him
or is it me, who would prefer
to keep on trembling.

Halloween Birches

Moonlight was silvering
the palm tree on my lawn.
It lit up the long arc of one frond.

After many years in California,
my first thought: A weeping birch?
I have a birch tree on my lawn?

And birch groves left behind a lifetime
ago came to me, bowed and flowed —
cloudy branches of that Celtic night

when the blindfold of time slips loose
and we see behind and beyond —
just as now that I can barely walk,

memories of mountain hikes
alight on my mind: Angel's Landing,
Never Summer, Dead Man's Pass.

Surprised by the brilliant crescent,
I walked on. The last of Halloween
children dressed as flame-red

devilkins or pink ballerina angels
were shooed by mothers into cars.
Only the souls of trees walked with me —

birches and beeches, maples, pines.
I whispered to them: *Remember me.*
They replied: *It's not important to be*

remembered — only to be beautiful.
The moon waited, a slender
canoe: *Get in, and not later but now.*

The Laughter of God

But the woman was growing restless.
You see, there was no
narrative. No verbs. Paradise is

pure description. No subjunctive
sighs and regrets,
no frolicking future tense.

When time like a ruddy fruit
hung from the branches of the galaxies,
I told the woman the truth

with the two-way tongue of a snake.
All those fluent ribs, opalescent
scales! It was Me undulating

in the subtle serpent.
Oh let them be as gods!
The multitudes of Me whirled

a wild polka through the nebulae:
At last! At last!
I've managed to create

beings able to disobey Me.
No, I didn't curse my
children. I blessed them.

To the woman I said,
"You are the Tree of Life."
To the man, "Love her, she'll be

your strength." Yes, I knew
suffering would happen.
Yes, because I love stories.

Paradise Revised

I'll tell you the Original Secret:
Adam and Eve never left
the Garden of Eden.
The Forbidden Fruit

wasn't an apple or a fig,
nor a primeval peach.
The name of the fruit was:
the Ideal.

They ate it and that day
they could imagine something better.

*

Old Moses knew what he was doing,
dying on scenic Mount Pisgah,
gazing from a safe distance
upon the Promised Land.

Miracle is not enough:
within a week,
the chosen people grumbled
about the taste of manna.

*

Pity poor King Solomon,
bored until he was wise
with his three hundred wives
and seven hundred concubines.

The Queen of Sheba
was not enough.
Not enough,
entering the promised flesh.

*

You see, they never left Eden,
the man and the woman,
the oldest story in the world.
Clouds billow into shapes

of animals yet unnamed.
The garden is here,
outside our window —
and the tree, and the golden snake.

Jonah Remembers the Whale

A rib arched above me.
Below the lungs blossomed,
the manifold cilia bowed.
I woke to humming, gurgling,
the mighty inner tides.

Lulled by the slush-slush
of the vast whale blood,
I felt washed clean of ego,
one with enveloping life.
No doomsday deadlines,

no burning graven images.
My heart murmur stilled
next to the giant heart
that tolled *Dive — dive —*

Then the command: "Out! Out!
Preach judgment unto
Nineveh!" Across the briny
irony of waves, weeping I waded
to loneliness again.

Now when twilight grows
on the roofs, hushes the palm
trees and bazaars, and the wind
in the tamarind grove
sighs like an old man,

I sit on the sand and dream
of the muffled green sun
of the sea; I ride the wild
forgiveness of the whale.

The Bela Lugosi Moth

In the hummingbird pavilion,
past an iridescent
veil of morpho butterflies,

wings not trembling nor folded
in prayer, but spread like a cape,
black silk, two yellow eyes —

the Bela Lugosi moth.

Bela, whose tombstone
I found in Los Angeles,
at the Cemetery of the Holy Cross.

Engraved in strict granite,
only name and dates —
slow syllables welling up,

in black flight swooping down,
in a crimson hush:
a shadow, a shudder, a hiss —

I mean *kiss* —

Do you cross this threshold
of your own free will?
the Count asks, we we must reply.

*

Bela, this moth is your true
memorial — something of you,
with black wings —

Fear too has its rituals, dresses
in capes and fastens fangs.
But when they taunt, *You never*

loved. You cannot love,
the vampire confesses,
I too can love —

a crucifixion, even as I linger
in the Hummingbird Pavilion,
happier than all the children

whose memory is daylight
and will self-destruct —
while I watch the Bela Lugosi

head-down on the false stone.
Taste is caution. Style is
daring. On black wings

the false eyes warn
art is love and will uncloak
hidden self you didn't know

waiting in the vivid dark,
the Great Undead
watching from the wall.

Non-Judgment Day

Here's what slipped into my heart:
that crested yellow tongue

down the runway of parched purple;
and the petals' pulsing blue,

the excitable color of now:
like coming on a meadow of wild iris.

Long ago in dank woods,
I blundered on a dell

of lilies-of-the valley:
white lovers palm to palm

between leaves. That's why God
must be forgiven, and why Dante puts

those who weep when they should
rejoice in a muddy pocket of hell

near the Wood of Suicides.
On Non-Judgment Day, in the Valley

of Saved Moments,
I will bloom, the wildest iris.

Paradise Anonymous

To me the Archangel came
not with a lily but a branch of flame.
In bed he covered me with wings
so soft I thought I'd drown.

If I roll over, I said, your wing
could break. He said those wings
were made of wishing on a star,
an astral amalgam.

Amalgam! My knees go weak.
I wade in liquid syllables.
Gabriel rustled in my sleep:
God makes love all the time,

his only interest is sex,
that's what comes of being immortal.
We have dying so we can transcend
the body's umber aftermath.

In memory of me, Gabriel said,
wear a silk slip like an embrace.
What matters in the end, he said,
is delinquent underwear —

the only heaven you will have,
unless you make it hell.
Black on black fire like the skin
of the ocean at night, I slip

into more slips than dresses now.
O little town of Bethlehem,
O little House of Bread or Breath,
how soft we let thee go.

New Year's Eve

Halfway on my evening walk
I saw headlights pass over the sage
in such hazy waves I thought: smoke —
someone set the hillside on fire.

When I left the house I was practicing
the mantra, I live in paradise.
Now I stood for a while, not sure.
The darkness descended, but not like a dove.

Still the ocean's giant breath
crept too close to let me forget.
Gloved with fog, I touched the world,
sticky burrs and silky stars.

Again it was paradise,
one more day as good as forever.

Mary to Jesus

Dearest Yeshu,
you don't visit, you don't write.
Do I even have a son?
I prepared a Passover seder;
all your brothers and sisters came.
Only your place stayed empty.
We waited for you as for Elijah.
Who do you think you are?
The Messiah?

It's my fault, I know.
Aunt Mattie used to say,
"You're raising this kid
as if he is God."
Now look at you —
your bones stick out,
your stomach's ruined with fast food.

Worse, I hear that you preach,
"Leave your mother and father,
your brother, sister, wife,
and follow me."
This in the name of God
who you claim is love.
What can anyone know
about forgiveness, love,
except from mother, brother,
father, sister, wife?

You want to practice what you preach?
Get married.
That would teach you more
than any fasting in the desert could.
You're over thirty now —
how come you only have male friends?
And the women who seek you out —
epileptics, sinners, and demoniacs.

People tell me you say,
Let the dead bury the dead.
Has my little boy gone mad?
Don't you know what family means?
That the room where we gather to eat
is the real Holy of Holies?

Yeshu dear, mothers preach
more than any rabbi ever will.
Mothers know that God is not
up there in blue void of heaven,
but right here with noise and smells.
When I'm cooking, there's more
religion in the kitchen
than in the temple on a Sabbath.

Or when it rains and your brother
holds his coat over his wife.
When your sister picks up a crying child.
My son, you said it yourself:
he who doesn't know love
cannot enter the Kingdom.

Yeshu, come soon. I'll cook lentil stew,
I'll bake honey cake
with my secret, a drop of bitters.
Yeshu, this meschugge idea
of having a mission from God
will only get you crucified.
That's what happens to the sons
who do not listen to their mothers.

For the Survivor

In honor of Edith Eger, survivor of Auschwitz, and all survivors of Auschwitz,
including my grandmother Veronika and my grandfather Yakub

If God lived on earth, people would break his windows.
— a Yiddish proverb

In a dream he heard a voice: *Socrates,*
make music — and Socrates
the unmusical, the mortal, wrote poems

while awaiting execution.
He said he didn't want to publish,
only to obey his dream. Do we believe

him, we who also write in
even stanzas as we await our execution,
deny we crave to publish and be

immortal; we're only obeying our dream.
But modern music favors dissonance:
percussive sound of being tossed

on piles of corpses, bone against bone,
pelvis against a shoulder blade; clavicle,
clavecin, a thousand years
to hose off this blood.

*

And when the angels come for us,
when time is ended, the trumpet's blast,
they'll say there's Hitler in all of us —

Yet we make music between the noise,
song will survive, look at my poise:
a cardboard sign around my neck,

name not my own, the glare of waves
curving and crashing, call it embrace;
reciting palm trees under my breath,

the platinum sheen of the Pacific
before all tenses shift to gold —
If God is Hitler we need to know,

the Tree of Knowledge obliges us.
Don't tell me poets lie too much,
Do not tell God he has the right to

remain silent. Love, can I borrow
your clarinet, that gurgling joy I dedicate
to the survivor who sings and laughs,

dances to live, for all of us.

*

Why would God bother with the Last Judgment:
bone joining bone, putting on flesh,
just to be judged? Redeemer, where?

She is among us, the one-time ballerina
behind the electric wire —
listen, she laughs, having survived

dancing for Doctor Mengele.
Her name is Edith, it means "blessed" —
like walking naked in a glass house,

safe from the stones that people throw,
thinking it's God's house; they shout
Heil Hitler and who could blame them,

they want to break his windows —
and those stones dancing,
and those stones bursting into stars.

Last Night of the Leonids

No moon. The pines like black wind
brushed the tips of stars.
Horses stood in their corral,
carved as if outside of time.

You said, "They are sleeping."
But one horse,
the tallest, suddenly
ran toward us, a rift in the dark.

The other horses never stirred.
They slept, eternal statues. Only he
sensed us and needed to see —
shot through darkness like a marble flame.

We almost stopped breathing, struck
with pure rhythm, muscle and mind —
that shining horse starting up —

then standing still,
the frost of stars
braiding his tall outline —

And we too stood still,
face to face,
in the shivering starlight.

II.

Let There Be Light

Eyeglasses

Before my grandparents left Auschwitz,
they went to the mountain of eyeglasses,
thinking that by a miracle
they might find their own.

But it was hopeless to sift
through thousands of tangled pairs.
They tried one pair after another.
They had nothing to read, so they traced

the wrinkles on their hands.
They'd bring the hand up close,
follow the orbits of knuckles,
the map of fate in the palm.

If one eye saw right,
the other was blurred.
Haze stammered the line of life.
They took several pairs.

My mother is embarrassed
telling me the story,
embarrassed her parents
took anything at all

from the piles of looted belongings.
But I would have been like them.
Those stripped to nothing end up
with too much, except nothing fits

after reading your hands
through the glasses of the dead—
This is how beauty looks
through those eyeglasses:

blurred, skeletal,
a man and a woman
help each other up,
lean on a handcart, walk on.

Passion Is Not Fire, but Surviving Fire

I felt indecent, coming to you
with so many scars —
the permanent necklace
around my throat,

scar at my lip, that kiss
gone wrong; slash on my knee,
rushing to please;
a death cry where memory starts.

Then we saw the giant
sequoias, carrying their
two thousand years,
every tree scarred by fire:

centuries of charred flesh.
Fallen logs spelled
what storm of roots
holds us in the earth.

In the morning I found you,
arms on a sequoia,
sun flaming branches,
tendrils of your hands —

on the trunk's other side,
a burn like a blazon,
hollow and black —
but the crown rising

into the green. We walked
among the surviving trees,
one after another
split to the root by lightning:

each scar an entrance
that could not be
entered, unspoken
in the green silence.

The High Diver

I'm trying to imagine you
diving, the water's fractured
net of lights
impossibly far
below —

the slender body
riding gravity,
arching and twisting,
folding and unfolding
in emptiness,

following the invisible
trajectory between
beginning and end,
making art of that delay.
But I want you

to tell me about
fear,
the water hardening
each second,
the emptiness

growing larger,
the body smaller,
more naked;
the tension climbing
step by step,

the prayer of deep breath,
the take-off —
and in falling
the feeling of
stillness.

The more you do
with your body,
the longer it seems to last —
when air becomes
first person,

sculpting the figure
between —
Then entry, like a child
going backwards, born
into the flesh of water;

the water licking you,
rocking you —
But I love most
the moment just before
the flight —

the narrow
second when you step
out of fear into the blue
dazzle of light
where the sky

bends,
then lets go.

Let There Be Light

My Aunt Henia,
learning her eighth language,
said that with every variety of speech
we gain a new soul. My souls are
fragmentary, small — a glimmer
from a candelabra in Versailles,

an echo of Caesar's laughter
wandering in Rome.
Snowdrifts bury me in Russian;
the Homeric sea
drowns my footprints
under the Arabian stars.

Gypsy aunt with your pack of souls,
meet me in the drizzle
at all the train stations.
With exquisite umlauts refined
in a German labor camp,
be my guide to a thousand mansions.

*

I am losing my tenses.
Grandmothers gossip
in dying dialects.
Italian flows back into Latin,
Lithuanian into Sanscrit —
into the mouth of the goddess
Sarasvati, the Flowing One,
Bringer of language.

I detested the story
of the Tower of Babel —
speech "confounded" as punishment.
Languages multiplied
because the universe
needed many mirrors of sound.

When I was eight I learned to ask
my father *Q'est-ce que c'est?*
Word by word he created the world.
The sun smiled into *soleil,*
the street wheeled into *la rue* —
the city glistened with vowels.

*

In a cloud-roofed lamastery,
Tibetan monks recite
the names of God.
After the last name is spoken,
the world is supposed to fall silent.

But isn't every word
a name of God? Flower, *kviat.*
Tree, *arbol.* Fire, *agni, fuego.*
Water, *voda, agua, mem.*
Turning in the tongues of flame,
the universe names itself.

I catch a spark of Hebrew:
Ayahi aur — "Let there be light."
My embryo Edenic soul
goes back to the beginning.
Vayahi aur — "And there was light."

Factories In Łódź

Sirens roared a hoarse hunger.
The walls thudded a thick pulse,
brick crusted with centuries of soot,
the looms' horizontal

music of massive shafts:
axis and thrust,
the surge and ebb of shuttles.
Behind the wire-paneled glass,

the quivering strings of cotton dust,
women in gray scarves like nuns
lifted their arms in fractured time
under rows of spidery lamps.

The old owners' names
over the wing-like gates
were supplanted with red-lettered signs:
"Lenin Thread Manufacture,"

"Textile Works
of the October Revolution."
But for me the factories
had no names as I passed

through the black-walled streets,
narcotic with ugliness and rhythm,
the knocking of returning shuttles:
More! More! Again! Again!

Multiple metal hearts
hammered my lullaby at night.
They repeated like an iron god:
I am that I am that I am.

But Not Like the Birds

We're here to sing, but not
like the birds. Brutal
science tells us only
the male sings, not for joy,

neither to praise God,
but to establish territory.
I me me mine, the nightingale
screams, his only lyrics.

We sing to trespass,
to cross boundaries.
To bring another world
into this world. Like the musicians

in the Warsaw Ghetto, who stood
in the starving streets and made
the most tender music they knew.
Like my father, paralyzed

with Parkinson's: when he could
barely speak, he began to sing
all the songs of his youth —
the last refugees he alone still knew.

After the autopsy the neurologist said
he'd never seen a brain so badly
destroyed: whole regions dead
like a bombed city.

A voice singing in the ruins
is the last to go.

The Gentleman

After the electric fence between
Auschwitz and Birkenau was switched off,
they found each other
alive, Veronika and Yakub —

my grandparents, skin drummed
against their bones.
They settled together in a barracks.
Veronika set off in search of food.

Near the warehouses she saw
three women inmates
herded by a Nazi.
As if on a whim, he shouted *Halt!*

and shot them all —
roared away on his motorcycle.
Veronika hid behind a waste bin;
afraid to pass by the bodies,

she started roundabout in the snow.
She stopped at a wide ditch.
On the other side came up a tall
blond man in civilian clothes.

He stretched out his arm
and pulled her across.
She warmly thanked him in Polish.
He nodded without a word.

And suddenly she saw:
this was an SS officer.
He'd taken off his
uniform, and was human.

What to Say to a Bear

Do not run. Stand still and talk softly to the bear.
— "What To Do If You Meet a Bear," Canadian National Park Service

Bear, you could make these bones
crack, you could spill into roots
my desire not to die.
How unhurried your tongue would be

burrowing into places
more secret than sex.
When you rise, you look
like a man — our image of terror.

We don't trust ourselves;
our sleep is shallow.
I should carry a bell like a leper.
I couldn't turn over rocks,

or paw the ground
with quartz-like claws;
it's difficult
for a human to be beautiful.

You climb into yourself for winter,
into your bulk and hoarded warmth.
I dream another birth,
licked with a long bear tongue.

Bear, give me a sign
the universe is kind;
its paws and shaggy nights embrace
the wilderness of human mind.

Bear, black luxury of the earth,
in truth I don't know
what I'd say. If talking softly
would be enough of an expiation.
Bear, pass me by. Another sky

begins in my silence.

In Los Angeles I Loved

coming up La Cienega Boulevard
on a clear winter day, when the cowl
of smog lifted, and snow-winged

mountains rose weightless beyond.
I drove toward that steep heaven,
obscured on polluted days

when La Cienega, whose name
means "mud," was a river in hell —
skeletal weeds on its banks,

the wheezing oil pumps;
bimbo billboards and tattoo parlors,
rusted grimy garages, discount

outlets piled with cheap clothes,
garish signs shouting in Spanish,
error-red exclamation marks.

But after lush winter rains,
a river of paradise
flowed amid the wildflowers,

millions of small laughing suns;
the oil pumps patient animals,
the rinsed garages platinum

harmonicas, poor but honest.
On a clear day, I trusted everyone.
I wanted the traffic to stop,

all to get out and kneel down.
No need for an afterlife:
snowy ghosts of the mountains

float above Los Angeles.
In the hidden sky,
clouds bloom like water lilies.

Barcelona

When I touched him there,
he felt delicate,
not the blatant maleness —

and I too grew delicate, discreet,
the female twin of Gemini
small enough to curl inside his palm.

Sometimes he was the small one —
I the maternal cello,
he the shimmering violin.

You have two selves, I said:
a lawyer with his exit
strategy, and Orpheus. And you

have two voices, he said,
a dark one from the Slavic woods,
and Hispanic, pitched to the bright

wine. *Barthelona*, I whispered,
to highlight European heritage,
but what of it, if Gaudi died

on a charity ward, insisting,
I belong here, among the poor —
And I belong nowhere, except

in brief arches of voices and hands:
the swell and dip of arm
and hip, the crescent of a smile,

but then La Sagrada
Familia will never be finished,
and only the body can curl

inside the music of another
body, and sleep.

Not Like Edith Piaf

Did anyone call her *petite*
when she sang — sparrow body
and that powerful voice,
a voice that had walked through hell.
How much she must have suffered
to regret nothing.

She sang *La vie en rose;* I waited
for the bus, thinking I too
could stand on the stage,
crucified in the lights,
singing youth's ignorant anthem:
I regret everything.

She sang *toujours l'amour.*
I knew I'd never find him,
transfigured into summer
and disaster —*l'amour*
life's deepest disappointment.
And art, a death-wish and delay.

She sang of Paris skies;
I stared at rusty garbage cans.
In my nightmares I was a waitress.
A friend said, *You could never
be a waitress. Your hands are too small.*

And I saw my passion
squandered in the kitchen,
in the classroom correcting commas –
saw I'd be not like Edith Piaf,
her tears those torrents of r's —

but here with my scribbled notes
stacked among shopping lists;
that mine would be
a way among shadows;
that I was already a soul

standing on the shore of Lethe,
refusing to forget;
wanting to recite by heart
the dark bread of childhood,
every shining crumb —

seeing by the arson glow
of history, family stories
long like smoke
threading the rhythmic
lace of bridges.

Love is eternal, she sings.
Her hands are too small.
We both know: between rubies
and a rose of live coals,
you reach for the burning embers.

Questions for God

I love deathbed stories.
Heisenberg allegedly said:
"I'm planning to pose
two questions to God:

why relativity, and why
chaos. I suspect
He'll be able to answer
the first one."

Most people aren't that deep.
Every day I prepare
a new question to pose to God,
though no doubt it's the same

question already asked
a trillion trillion times,
and in vain. All my life I have sought
a science-compatible God,

friendly and kidding around,
like scientists at a gerontology convention.
But the I-Am-That-I-Am
will speak to me neither

from a burning bush,
nor from the serpent space-time
curving back on itself —
In the neural branches

of my Tree of Knowledge,
I already suspect
God will have my mother's
face, and will greet me

in the doorway of a nebula
in her usual way:
"Take off that awful blouse at once,
and put on something pretty."

My Mother Asks Me Not To Write About WWII

"Why write about this old stuff?"
Not for this she gave me life.
Not for this she sent me
to the country of the future.

"Hitler is dead," she says.
She remembers that night —
The chill, uncertain May
has just begun. She's not in

ruined Warsaw, but in her leafy
home town, sleeping,
when church bells wake her up,
ringing loud and wild.

Lights go on in the windows,
people rush into streets,
women in coats over nightgowns
moon-shadowed, glancing,

whispering. Someone shouts:
"Hey, these are wedding
bells!" A few men run
back in to listen to the radio —

the Red Army entered
Hitler's bunker, found
two bodies partly burned:
Hitler and Eva Braun.

The bells sway the stunned air.
Neighbors and strangers
embrace, kiss on both cheeks,
laugh and weep. *Hitler is*

dead, is dead, is dead,
the bells ring all over town,
and the difficult future begins —
wedding bells in the dark.

Azrael

"Polish or German, what's the difference,"
he shrugged, the American
who thought I was German.
"A huge difference," I began,

face flushed with the venom of history.
Dates of battles,
marshes of blood.
I grew up in a mass graveyard.

Yet the stranger was right.

No nation is eternal.
Greece keens over the splendid
broken bodies;
Egypt sleeps in her own tomb.

Who I really was —
Polish or German,
French or Russian —
empty thrones in echoing museums.

*

On my second trip to Poland, we visited
my mother's schoolteacher.
Ninety-four, she'd grown tiny as a child,
her skin peeling like an old oilcloth.

Straining to see us,
her eyes bleached of color,
she fluttered to the oak wardrobe:
"Oh, I must put on something pretty!"

She recognized only my cousin
Janka, the daughter of her
great love. Told over and over
who I was, whose daughter I was,

she'd forget and greet me again,
looking up with such light
in those half-blind eyes
that slowly I understood:

what my name was,
whose daughter I was —
echoes thinner
than the soul.

When the Angel of Love and Death
stands over us
with trembling wings,
no difference as she sings

another story. It's the music
that carries us on.

Verloren

My first memory of German
six years old, running
through our Łodź apartment
chanting *Heil Hitler*
Hände hoch

petrified parents
plucking the exotic
bloodied syllables
from my happy mouth

but when I was sixteen
my neighbor from Silesia
called me *Fräulein Yoasia*

she taught me the caress of umlauts
long journeys of *Wehmut*
leiden and *verloren*
that music of sorrow

I stood under those vowels
as in a petal-fall

Ich bin verloren I whispered
in secret to myself
in the language of the enemy
described all around me
as "subhuman barking"

*

What *verloren* means
a Mazurian village
the blond bowing of the wheat
a woman opens the door

on the table she puts
milk and honey
home-churned butter
bread fragrant with the sun

white lace blooms
in the windows
saints on the
lime-washed wall

*

Memory is a translation
from a dead language

she waits for us forever
that shimmering young girl

lost mouths that kiss us
as we pass

The Signal

I'd listen to his heart, and he to mine —
one thing we did in bed,

as if needing to receive a signal
of another life, naked and equally

endangered. He must have
forgotten that sound when he

pressed the gun to his temple,
not quite twenty-nine. He had

a Russian revolutionary look;
his hair refused to stay down,

tense and alive, prickling my fingertips
months after his burial.

My hands remember the hushed
prayer of opening his shirt,

the liturgy of each button.
I'd kiss his left nipple, undo

more buttons, kiss the right one —
slyly dip my tongue in his navel.

Then we listened to each other's
heart — though my mind

mistranslated every systole,
diastole as the survivor's

loves me, while his rhythm
repeated *loves me not*.

Words for Snow

I begin to count the words for snow
in the singing languages I know,
but can't wade past the first one,

śnieg — a grandmother word —
fairy tale of my life
with wolves in it. Tiny needles of fate

stitch my face, my eyes.
La neige, I think, and am saved —
the way he could say

Je t'aime, but never
"I love you." What he loved
was the elegant scar

of my accent. He and I
in the hollow of his car
talk without touching until I

whisper goodbye. I watch
the ghost glide
of my hand over his; he laces

his fingers with mine —
We press into each other's arms,
try to kiss, but cannot —

our lips will not stick,
our mouths are too dry.
We let go in a darker dark,

do not know who we are:
he the bridegroom of death,
my miraculous error,

my own season in hell
I'll walk out of — not his
bride, but my own.

*

If I were again in that car,
again young and starved,
could I say with an artist's

absolute, hardened heart:
Go ahead, kill yourself,
make me a poet —

No — I want only
that moment of failure,
going into a darker dark —

Grandmother in frost-lily stars,
teach me how to pray for the dead.
She answers: "Plant flowers."

First Anniversary, Colorado

I stray into an aspen grove,
among trees like brides —
white trunks with black scars
left by the missing branches.
Some say, if at sixteen

we could see our future life,
none of us would choose
to live. But I would have.
Because aspen leaves
turn silver in the wind.

Where is he — the other one,
the man I was waiting
for him to become —
now he wavers behind
every shimmering tree.

Over the eastern peaks,
the sky blackens with storm.
The lightning practices
its writing on the granite wall.
It was the mountains

in him that I loved,
not the man who said,
People will despise you
for having wasted
yourself on me.

And that was youth.
Now the woman
I was waiting to become
walks with thunder,
the delayed echo.

Music

Ten years after your suicide,
this is the moment I love best:
in silence you take my hand
and put your arm around my waist.

In narrow steps, as though
on a crowded dance floor, we turn
and sway, our rhythm perfect,
the same silence leading us both.

We turn in tight circles,
we are almost formal. No
kissing, no: we dance as if
still only dreaming of each other.

We feel each other's breathing,
our bodies' boundaries of warmth.
Slowly we dance without music –
unless *we* are the music –

How else can I explain
that in such silence we do not hear
the shot that travels farther and farther
into the past, while we dance.

Aldebaran

The only philosophical
question left,
a French philosopher said,
is whether to kill yourself.

But that is the question of youth.
In my twenties, I could never look
from a high window or a roof
and not feel a gathering leap.

Middle age asks two questions:
How much time left? and
*How to spend what wakefulness
remains?* Now I look out the window,

and the deep magnolia
gives two answers:
the morning light
glistening in the crown,

and the wreath of shadow.
And the layered wind
does not rustle youth's *To be
or not to be.* Each leaf remembers

Hamlet's forgotten reply:
Let be. It's too late to renounce
the privilege of surprise;
centuries, it seems,

since my father told me
not to worry about the universe.
"That's Aldebaran," he pointed
to an amber star.

When the universe shall ask
the final question, I too
will point: *Aldebaran.*
Great light seen only in the dark.

Asphodel

When his darkness seized me,
the great love of my youth,
when I dared to reach for the most

magnificent narcissus,
the earth opened and horses
rearing like black smoke

carried me off to marry
the Invisible Lord —
so my song would be both

ravishing and true.
Because love has two flowers:
narcissus and asphodel.

A hundred-headed narcissus!
We grow of many minds.
A hundred wishes, ten thousand —

and echo has the last word.
Narcissus — flower of youth,
rippling into departure.

Asphodel swaying in no wind,
in twilight memory of sun,
you have no scent except

in the mind that remembers.
Asphodel, flower of soul,
of love at the ripe hour:

the ancients understood
the soul feeds on flowers.
Even in hell,

a life filled with flowers.
After trails of sunny narcissi,
I walk in mothlike meadows.

Archaic Penelope

It's my waiting that creates you.
The tapestry I weave,
unraveling you in dreams,
is your secret map.

How you try
to read over my shoulder!
You're too close,
thinking you are too far.

Here's a seaweed-dripping cave
and a sea-nymph's bribe:
immortality, but nothing else
will ever happen in your life —

and you pick mortality,
that beautiful blood flower.
At the cold mouth of the earth,
the dead greet you, arms of mist —

like an echo of the future
in their shroud of finished past.
On the Island of Lament,
there's no pain at Circe's trough;

and above the ledge of bones,
the Sirens unriddle all.
Days slide off the loom of hours.
Again you dream of home.

Wreathed with horizons,
you want me
to stroke your neck,
stiff from looking ahead;

weary of women
opening like shores,
you want my body to lead
into the body of silence.

You beg to know
how the story ends —
and it is I
who tie you to the mast.

David

He meets me at the train station.
A smile dances in his open face,
his elegant lean body.
More than I ever

loved anyone, I love
my son in my dream —
the lost amber of his eyes,
marble cross of shoulders.

How do I know it would have
been a son? A mother knows,
I say, I who have no right
to call myself a mother.

We walk through a quiet town
dripping with lilacs, peonies.
Is it Pomerania where I was born,
its cathedrals of clouds,

misty Eden of the Yvelines,
river-rich Hungary —
No, these are the Mourning
Fields, the green

country of that other
memory, rainy mirror
of what didn't happen.
How lonely I've been.

We step on a rain-beaded porch.
As always, he disappears.
And these words, this parched
paradise, what is it
if not

the life he has given me.

Gripper

Mother and I pried open the bronze,
divided his ashes between us.
I took my portion upstairs,
quickly closed the door.

I felt queasy. I had never seen
human ashes before —
would they still look human,
with sharp pieces of offended bone?

But my father's ashes
looked just like ashes:
gray, speckled with white.
Then I glimpsed something

round and hard: a metal button.
On the disk, legible still,
the word *Gripper* twice —
two serpents made of letters,

smudged but not charred —
not returning dust to dust.
Soon I found more Grippers,
from his cremated hospital gown.

With half the ashes, half
the Grippers were later laid
in the family crypt
in my father's hometown —

blessed by the priest,
consigned to everlasting mercy.
As if a sprinkling of holy water
could extinguish such persistent flame.

During the service, in my mind
I heard my father ask: "Is that
what is left of me? Buttons?
That's the treasure you found?"

"Not worth a button"
was his favorite saying.
Laughter was his grip on life.
Only days before the end,

he said, with his widest grin,
"When you're lying
in the coffin, you should suddenly
sit up and say *Hah-hah!*"

That was of course too ambitious.
From eternity I have only
these buttons. Still able
to grip. Not giving up.

Crossing San Andreas

Frazier Park, California

Cosmo, my neighbor, who believed
that rocks have consciousness,
they are just slow,
showed me at last where lay

the San Andreas Earthquake Fault:
"Right here. It's the river."
He meant the muddy trickle
meandering through sagebrush —

the bridge that spanned it ran
a quarter of a block. Each time
I crossed the bridge, I crossed
from the Pacific Plate

to the North American Plate.
I slept and worked and hiked
among the piñon pines
on the Pacific Plate; I crossed

to the North American Plate to shop.
The market was there,
the drugstore. I had to have
both tectonic plates.

Cosmo said, "When the next
earthquake hits,
half of here will shear
toward San Francisco;

the other half will slide
down toward Baja."
San Francisco or Baja?
I had to have both.

Isn't everyone always
crossing from world to world?
Ecstasy, or the laundry?
The soul too is a housewife

and requires both.
From parent to teacher
to artist, from I love you
to oil for the salad,

fissures, earthquake faults,
a bridge where you drop
your name like a lost coin —
knowing any instant

a shudder could start,
half of you leap north,
half of you slide south.
The last earthquake,

Cosmo explained,
took place two hundred
years ago. Great oaks
snapped like saplings,

rifts opened ten feet wide.
Cosmo wasn't afraid:
"I built the house myself.
I put in the best

studs and bolts."
I admired this male faith
in studs and bolts,
though I felt shaken myself,

every day stepping across
from the Pacific Plate
to the North American Plate.
The earthquake was

overdue, but rocks
have a different sense of time.
Now and then one could spot
a seismologist up the slope

with his long-legged
instruments, his metal
measuring rod —
the sky flawless, lilacs

drunk with blossoms,
rocks thinking
their stone thoughts,
the pressure building up.

Bride of the Wind

It was a dream of heaven: I was in my bed,
and the green-eyed motorcycle rider I met
in the Mazurian Lakes, and waited for
that whole year, walking the leafy

length of Warsaw, found me at last —
this bridegroom of the wind,
his weight the sweet burden
of everything unknown.

Only now, too late, I know
America will not make you happy,
nor publications, nor awards.
That night again I heard

the music of what never happened,
though it did: he came to me
in my other life, the one unlived
in the country I'd left.

In that heaven thin as the mist
that breathes on All Hallows'
graves, I had no plans:
I only wanted to feel

his body on top of my body.
In the music that would never stop
we lay dreamless in the quiet dark,
far from time, not needing anything.

Often I Am Permitted to Return to a Meadow

in blue-green Carpathia, just to hear
a rooster crow —
then the echo — and reply —

and far away,
as if hung in high blue air,
another pure return —

an echo for each meadow,
in a widening ring.
The echo of all the roosters I heard

in those Carpathian summers still
travels from hill to hill.
By now it has reached Krakow,

bending around the blue-green
copper domes and tombs of kings,
where the Vistula embraces

the city like shining laughter,
like a gleaming wheel.
And the echo travels

as starlight can travel
for a thousand years —
and we wish on a dead star

that still guides us here.
So the echoes of us roll
in a widening ring —

of the song we sang,
and thought
that we were not heard.

Saint Joan Speaks To Me

I'm walking down the cobbled
streets of Rouen. Cabbage leaves
blacken in the gutter.
In the square they are burning

Joan of Arc. Her eyes are
transparent with light.
She says, *Truth is a torch.*
but it makes a beautiful blaze.

The crowd is weeping.
Her lips are charred
doors of light. She says,
A dead body is only a dead body.

How can we tell soul from ash
unless we too rise,
a blue heron of smoke
slanting into flight—

that pulse of a wing so slow,
so soaring when she says,
We are all burning.
Be a brighter fire.

April Snow

I climb to Condor Lookout
into snowdrifts of clouds.
To what altar do we wade,
white procession with snow-lit pine?

That night a beautiful young man
dawns at my door
with a rifle, a soldier's uniform.
He smiles a boyish smile.

I don't seduce, I don't plead.
I chat: where is he from, is he happy.
I want what little time is left
to have tenderness.

He is the age my son would be,
if I had a son — this handsome
executioner, life's last gift,
like the trees shining in crystal.

Over his shoulder I see
the slopes sparkle with moist breath.
His smile covers everything.
Don't worry, I say, I know.

I show him my daily list,
little whips of chores;
my walk before sunset,
when the light is the best.

But with petals of April snow
the wind has erased my tracks.
Pines and firs go with me.
I only want tenderness.

Listening to Gabriela Read in Spanish

La noche es infinita, she begins.
What is born in her mouth
slides out slippery like moonlight —

her name a Hebrew archangel
translated into a woman
creating herself. I pour infinity

into my native tongue,
let it create another world:
The night is not finished.

The night is not finished, it waits
behind the unfinished trees,
it makes the dogs bark and coyotes

laugh. What do they hear that we
cannot hear? *Infinidad*, she says because
we're infinite but we are not

finished. The Universe is mostly
dark laced with dark,
pierced by the cry of the beginning.

There's space like a lover
that opens only once. Gabriela
waits, a lily in her hand.

What will you say to her?
Can you utter such a total Yes?
Do not ask if the angel

is real. Who wants a heaven
that is always day? We need
la noche, our native land,

black *leche* of the soul,
white of stars

Moje Serce

You ask me to tell you
some love words in Polish

I hesitate
afraid you might not like
the hard *h* in the verb for love

but you lie still and trusting
as though expecting an unknown
caress

*mój miły mój złoty
mój aniele —*

It's California January
sun beats on the pillow
I take you to the country
of first snow

protected by a language
you cannot enter
I coo the extravagant
catalogue

I call you *moje serce*
my heart

That's what I want you to be
at night before falling asleep
I repeat the brief
syllable of your name

this will end but the story
does not give us up

the room snowy with light
I whisper *moje serce* and you
whisper back
it sounds wonderful go on

About the Author

Oriana Ivy was born in Poland and came to the United States when she was 17. Her poems, essays, book reviews, and translations have been published in *Poetry, Ploughshares, Best American Poetry, Nimrod, Spoon River Review, The Iowa Review, Black Warrior Review, Los Angeles Review of Books* and many others. She's the prize winning author of the chapbooks *April Snow* (Finishing Line Press), *From a New World* (Paper Nautilus), and *How to Jump from a Moving Train* (Cervena Barva). *Paradise Anonymous* (Moon Tide Press) is her first full-length collection. A former journalist and community college instructor, she leads an online Poetry Salon. Her poetry-and-culture blog, oriana-poetry.blogspot.com, has gained an international audience. She lives in Southern California.

Acknowledgements

Angel Envy — *April Snow* (chapbook, Finishing Line Press, 2012)

Jonah Remembers the Whale – *HMS Beagle*

Crossing San Andreas — Sheila-Na-Gig

An Apple Tree for Osip Mandelstam — *The Iowa Review*

The Guardians — *Knot*

The High Diver — *The Crucible*

Our Lady of the Third Arm — *Psychological Perspectives*

Paradise Revised — *Zone 3*

Aldebaran — *Knot* (online, Pushcart nomination)

Azrael — *Mudfish*

Bear (What to Say to a Bear) — *San Diego Poetry Annual, 2015*

Eyeglasses — *The Exquisite Corpse, Best American Poetry*

Factories in Łódź — *Poetry*

Let There Be Light — *Nebraska Review*

My Mother Asks Me — *Los Angeles Review*

Passion Is Not Fire — *Plainsong*

Saint Joan Speaks to Me — *Qarrtziluni*

Also Available from Moon Tide Press

Maze Mouth, Brian Sonia-Wallace (2023)
Tangled by Blood, Rebecca Evans (2023)
Another Way of Loving Death, Jeremy Ra (2023)
Kissing the Wound, J.D. Isip (2023)
Feed It to the River, Terhi K. Cherry (2022)
Beat Not Beat: An Anthology of California Poets Screwing on the Beat and Post-Beat Tradition (2022)
When There Are Nine: Poems Celebrating the Life an Achievements of Ruth Bader Ginsburg (2022)
The Knife Thrower's Daughter, Terri Niccum (2022)
2 Revere Place, Aruni Wijesinghe (2022)
Here Go the Knives, Kelsey Bryan-Zwick (2022)
Trumpets in the Sky, Jerry Garcia (2022)
Threnody, Donna Hilbert (2022)
A Burning Lake of Paper Suns, Ellen Webre (2021)
Instructions for an Animal Body, Kelly Gray (2021)
Head *V* Heart: New & Selected Poems, Rob Sturma (2021)
Sh!t Men Say to Me: A Poetry Anthology in Response to Toxic Masculinity (2021)
Flower Grand First, Gustavo Hernandez (2021)
Everything is Radiant Between the Hates, Rich Ferguson (2020)
When the Pain Starts: Poetry as Sequential Art, Alan Passman (2020)
This Place Could Be Haunted If I Didn't Believe in Love, Lincoln McElwee (2020)
Impossible Thirst, Kathryn de Lancellotti (2020)
Lullabies for End Times, Jennifer Bradpiece (2020)
Crabgrass World, Robin Axworthy (2020)
Contortionist Tongue, Dania Ayah Alkhouli (2020)
The only thing that makes sense is to grow, Scott Ferry (2020)
Dead Letter Box, Terri Niccum (2019)
Tea and Subtitles: Selected Poems 1999-2019, Michael Miller (2019)
At the Table of the Unknown, Alexandra Umlas (2019)
The Book of Rabbits, Vince Trimboli (2019)
Everything I Write Is a Love Song to the World, David McIntire (2019)
Letters to the Leader, HanaLena Fennel (2019)
Darwin's Garden, Lee Rossi (2019)
Dark Ink: A Poetry Anthology Inspired by Horror (2018)
Drop and Dazzle, Peggy Dobreer (2018)

Junkie Wife, Alexis Rhone Fancher (2018)
The Moon, My Lover, My Mother, & the Dog, Daniel McGinn (2018)
Lullaby of Teeth: An Anthology of Southern California Poetry (2017)
Angels in Seven, Michael Miller (2016)
A Likely Story, Robbi Nester (2014)
Embers on the Stairs, Ruth Bavetta (2014)
The Green of Sunset, John Brantingham (2013)
The Savagery of Bone, Timothy Matthew Perez (2013)
The Silence of Doorways, Sharon Venezio (2013)
Cosmos: An Anthology of Southern California Poetry (2012)
Straws and Shadows, Irena Praitis (2012)
In the Lake of Your Bones, Peggy Dobreer (2012)
I Was Building Up to Something, Susan Davis (2011)
Hopeless Cases, Michael Kramer (2011)
One World, Gail Newman (2011)
What We Ache For, Eric Morago (2010)
Now and Then, Lee Mallory (2009)
Pop Art: An Anthology of Southern California Poetry (2009)
In the Heaven of Never Before, Carine Topal (2008)
A Wild Region, Kate Buckley (2008)
Carving in Bone: An Anthology of Orange County Poetry (2007)
Kindness from a Dark God, Ben Trigg (2007)
A Thin Strand of Lights, Ricki Mandeville (2006)
Sleepyhead Assassins, Mindy Nettifee (2006)
Tide Pools: An Anthology of Orange County Poetry (2006)
Lost American Nights: Lyrics & Poems, Michael Ubaldini (2006)

Patrons

Moon Tide Press would like to thank the following people for their support in helping publish the finest poetry from the Southern California region. To sign up as a patron, visit www.moontidepress.com or send an email to publisher@moontidepress.com.

Anonymous
Robin Axworthy
Conner Brenner
Nicole Connolly
Bill Cushing
Susan Davis
Kristen Baum DeBeasi
Peggy Dobreer
Kate Gale
Dennis Gowans
Alexis Rhone Fancher
HanaLena Fennel
Half Off Books & Brad T. Cox
Donna Hilbert
Jim & Vicky Hoggatt
Michael Kramer
Ron Koertge & Bianca Richards
Gary Jacobelly
Ray & Christi Lacoste
Jeffery Lewis
Zachary & Tammy Locklin
Lincoln McElwee
David McIntire
José Enrique Medina
Michael Miller & Rachanee Srisavasdi
Michelle & Robert Miller
Ronny & Richard Morago
Terri Niccum
Andrew November
Jeremy Ra
Luke & Mia Salazar
Jennifer Smith
Roger Sponder
Andrew Turner
Rex Wilder
Mariano Zaro
Wes Bryan Zwick